NASUTOCERATOPS

BY REBECCA SABELKO

EPIC

BELLWETHER MEDIA • MINNEAPOLIS, MN

EPIC BOOKS are no ordinary books. They burst with intense action, high-speed heroics, and shadows of the unknown. Are you ready for an Epic adventure?

This edition first published in 2022 by Bellwether Media, Inc.

No part of this publication may be reproduced in whole or in part without written permission of the publisher. For information regarding permission, write to Bellwether Media, Inc., Attention: Permissions Department, 6012 Blue Circle Drive, Minnetonka, MN 55343.

Library of Congress Cataloging-in-Publication Data

Names: Sabelko, Rebecca, author.
Title: Nasutoceratops / by Rebecca Sabelko.
Description: Minneapolis, MN : Bellwether Media, 2022. | Series: The world of dinosaurs |
Includes bibliographical references and index. | Audience: Ages 7-12 | Audience: Grades 2-3 |
Summary: "Engaging images accompany information about nasutoceratops. The combination of
    high-interest subject matter and light text is intended for students in grades 2 through 7"-- Provided by publisher.
Identifiers: LCCN 2021022417 (print) | LCCN 2021022418 (ebook) | ISBN 9781644875452 (library binding) |
    ISBN 9781648345012 (paperback) | ISBN 9781648344534 (ebook)
Subjects: LCSH: Centrosaurus--Juvenile literature.
Classification: LCC QE862.O65 S2385 2022 (print) | LCC QE862.O65 (ebook) | DDC 567.915--dc23
LC record available at https://lccn.loc.gov/2021022417
LC ebook record available at https://lccn.loc.gov/2021022418

Editor: Betsy Rathburn   Designer: Jeffrey Kollock

Printed in the United States of America, North Mankato, MN.

TABLE OF CONTENTS

THE WORLD OF THE NASUTOCERATOPS

The nasutoceratops was a huge dinosaur! It is known for its large nose.

The dinosaur lived around 75 million years ago. This was during the Late **Cretaceous period** of the **Mesozoic era**.

MAP OF THE WORLD

Late Cretaceous period

NAME GAME

Nasutoceratops means "big-nose horned face."

PRONUNCIATION

na-SU-toe-SAIR-uh-TOPS

WHAT WAS THE NASUTOCERATOPS?

The nasutoceratops weighed around 5,000 pounds (2,268 kilograms). That is about the size of a rhino!

The dinosaur was around 15 feet (4.6 meters) long. Its head alone was about 5 feet (1.5 meters) long!

SIZE CHART

15 feet (4.6 meters)

10 feet (3 meters)

5 feet (1.5 meters)

Long horns stuck out above the dinosaur's eyes. A large **frill** curved around the back of its head. Scientists believe the horns and frill were mostly used to show off to **mates**.

horn

frill

DIET AND DEFENSES

beak

The nasutoceratops was a plant eater. Its hard beak helped it pull leaves from tough plants.

Its jaws were filled with hundreds of teeth. They formed a **dental battery**. The battery chopped plants into small pieces.

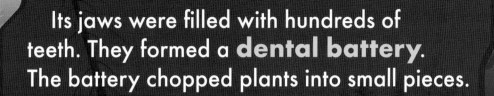

⚠ NEW TEETH

The nasutoceratops did not have the same teeth for its entire life. Old teeth fell out when they became dull. New teeth grew in their place!

⚠ NASUTOCERATOPS DIET

shrubs

leafy plants

The nasutoceratops was likely too slow to outrun **predators**.

Scientists think the dinosaur lived in a **herd**. The herd may have helped keep the dinosaur safe.

herd

Sometimes the dinosaur had to fight. It locked horns with other nasutoceratops to fight for mates.

It also fought off predators. Its wide frill protected its neck from deadly bites.

FOSSILS AND EXTINCTION

A huge **meteorite** crashed into Earth around 66 million years ago. It caused Earth to change. The nasutoceratops could not survive the disaster. It went **extinct**.

The first nasutoceratops **fossils** were found in Utah in 2006. Scientists hope to find more fossils in the future.

model of a nasutoceratops skull

⚠️ IN THE MOVIES!

The nasutoceratops is in the short movie *Jurassic World: Battle at Big Rock.*

Canada

United States

Mexico

More discoveries will help scientists learn even more about the nasutoceratops!

GET TO KNOW THE NASUTOCERATOPS

large nose

frill

horns

beak

HEIGHT around 5 feet (1.5 meters) tall at the shoulder

⚠️ **FOUND BY**

Eric Lund

⚠️ **LOCATION**

North America

LENGTH about 15 feet (4.6 meters) long

⚠ ERA

100 million to 66 million years ago during the Late Cretaceous period

Mesozoic era

Triassic	Jurassic	Cretaceous

⚠ FIRST FOSSILS FOUND

2006 in Utah, USA

⚠ FOOD

leafy plants

shrubs

⚠ WEIGHT

around 5,000 pounds (2,268 kilograms)

GLOSSARY

Cretaceous period—the last period of the Mesozoic era that happened between 145 million to 66 million years ago; the Late Cretaceous period began around 100 million years ago.

dental battery—a group of hundreds of tightly packed teeth that work together to grind tough plants

extinct—no longer living

fossils—the remains of living things that lived long ago

frill—a bony fan at the back of a nasutoceratops's head

herd—a group of dinosaurs that lived and traveled together

mates—pairs of adult animals that produce babies

Mesozoic era—a time in history in which dinosaurs lived on Earth; the first birds, mammals, and flowering plants appeared on Earth during the Mesozoic era.

meteorite—a space rock that hits Earth

predators—animals that hunt other animals for food

TO LEARN MORE

AT THE LIBRARY

Braun, Eric. *Could You Survive the Cretaceous Period?: An Interactive Prehistoric Adventure.* North Makato, Minn.: Capstone Press, 2020.

Lessem, Don. *Ultimate Dinopedia: The Most Complete Dinosaur Reference Ever.* Washington, D.C.: National Geographic, 2017.

Sabelko, Rebecca. *Triceratops.* Minneapolis, Minn.: Bellwether Media, 2020.

ON THE WEB

FACTSURFER

Factsurfer.com gives you a safe, fun way to find more information.

1. Go to www.factsurfer.com.

2. Enter "nasutoceratops" into the search box and click Q.

3. Select your book cover to see a list of related content.

INDEX